Pieces of Me

Arna Kerklaan

Presentation by *BookLeaf Publishing*

Web: www.bookleafpub.com

E-mail: info@bookleafpub.com

ISBN: 9789357212168

First edition 2023

I dedicate this to my family, my friends and my clients.

Those that show up, that trust in me, believe in me, understand me, connect with me and give me purpose, meaning and direction each day to keep believing in me, and doing what I do best.

ACKNOWLEDGEMENT

I would like to acknowledge all of those that have come before me, that have shaped my path and paved my way, to having strong morals and values and a vision filled with meaning and making a difference.

Those that have shown me what it truely is to have compassion, to see the good in each person and each day, to know the value in giving blessings to what is right before me.

To know that your knowledge and skills are but gifts to share and not to hold onto..... They are what give you purpose and connection, and from this the vulnerability to turn up and just be you, regardless of how you are feeling.

To my family thank you for showing me this!

PREFACE

I hope you find pieces of yourself through the pieces of me that are on these pages and remember the depth of your feelings and that the journey is meant to be felt, for it is only through the struggles and hard times that we realise the determination, gratitude and strength that exists in us each day.

Hope Tries

Get up, fall down, and get back up again,
You fight to survive and face what's around the
bend.
The Fear of failure, that keeps pushing through,
that despite your best efforts, still seems to
hinder what you do.

You try and you try, but with each attempt, you
crack,
Starting to feel like you'll never find your way
back.
The battle inside of heart, mind and soul,
Wears you so thin, it feels like it's taken its toll.

Stretched thin beyond recognition of who you
used to be,
of the life, lived with passion, purpose and
integrity.
But if you stop and truly listen, hand over your
heart and really try,
you'll start to notice, those pieces of you that
haven't said goodbye.

They're just hiding in the wings, waiting for their
2nd call,
and you choose to let them back in or let the
curtain fall.
The choice of how each act ends is entirely up to
you
and when you see it's not the end, that's when
you break back through!

This is just the lull point, before the next action
and excitement begins,
and you decide whether the main character
gets defeated, persists or wins.
When we look inside ourselves and see the
values inside,
It's no longer a fearful journey, but one with
fulfilment and pride.

It is knowing with Hope and with dreams in
your heart,
that every up and down is a lesson, it's not the
final part.
Please step into the light and embrace the
rehearsal,
because hope leads you forward and stops the
negative reversal.

Visions

Sometimes your vision is clear and direct,
Value-aligned, you know what to expect.
But unless you live your life, with your vision in direction,
You'll only end up with regret, when you finally sit in reflection.

Through your eyes

How hard it can be through the eyes of yourself,
when you've already placed yourself at the back
of the shelf.
What you see is failure, inadequacy and doubt,
feeling empty, heavy, you're silenced,
You laugh, then cry or you'll only shout.

You cannot see through this clouded vision of
you,
that says you're inadequate in all that you do.
Feeling powerless, hopeless, worthless, your
only thoughts of you.
Feeling messed up in the head, such a cloudy
view,

Through clouded judgement and only eyes of
despair
Seeing only your worst self as not worthy of
care.
Feeling not worthy of respect, love or belonging,
pushing yourself away, internalising your
longing…

When you feel like this, I hope you close your
eyes,
and see the vision of you, through those
passerbyes.
The way they see your eyes and your deep
longing for connection,
the way you turn up and keep fighting,
despite feeling a lack of direction

The way in the eyes of others, you are
determined and strong
and what you see through your own eyes, is a
lie, it is wrong.
When you feel like this I hope that you see,
your passion, hope, integrity and love
And don't forget after every dark cloud, it is the
sun that still rises above.

I wish

If your world has changed and you don't know
what to do,
Today I wish you clarity, to take little steps to
get you through.

If your world seems paused and you feel stuck
inside,
Today I wish you gratitude, and learning to ebb
and flow like the tide.

If your world is feeling like it is crumbling in on
you,
Today I wish you peace, in you and all the things
you do.

If your world has collided and you feel that you
are stuck,
Today I wish you perseverance, in knowing all
you do isn't just luck.

Trust you are enough

When the world feels like it's against you,
and the sea seems too rough...
Believe you've got the strength to sail through,
Trust you are enough.

When life suddenly hits you
and everything seems too tough...
Believe that your determination will get you
through,
Trust you are enough.

When you've got every opportunity before you,
and your brain tries to call your bluff.
Believe your vision but focus on the journey
through,
Trust you are enough!

Stop, Listen, Hear

Stop
Listen
Hear!

Do you really hear?
The beating of your heart,
it's longing and desire?
Or do you hear all the things
that just make you tire?

Do you really hear?
The whisper of your heart,
Its purpose and its yearning?
Or do you hear regret and failure,
that stop you from progressing and learning?

Do you really hear?
The music of your heart,
The clear vision that drives you to start?
Or do you hear your fear over logic
and hide away not playing your part?

Do you really hear?

STOP
LISTEN
HEAR!

Remember the Trees

Today I hope you listen to the desire of your
heart…
As it speaks like the wind through the rustle of
the leaves.

Today I hope you feel and see the needs of your
heart…
As a voice, it is given, through the bend and the
wane of the trees.

Today I hope you hear the quiet whisper of your
heart…
As firm roots it has built, to ride the up and
downs of life seas.

Today I hope you see all the beauty in your
heart…
As the sun sets on the forest, find warmth in all
your heart believes.

Clouded view

Everywhere I look,
I see something to do,
It blurs my vision and
clouds my view,
It does not get me any closer
to what I really want to do!

Clouds... I'm breaking through!

Overloaded

Sensory overload, you hear everything in sight
the birds, the cars, the buzz of the computer, the
tick of the clock to your right.

Unable to focus, concentrate or sit still,
It feels like everything wants your attention...
you must listen against your will.

Louder and Louder the sounds around you get,
That you can't even write because the sound on
the paper now makes you fret.

Can't sit still, Can't listen, Concentrate, NO!
I can't, it won't stop, can't sit still, everything
tells me to go…

Then they yell or they look, they taunt and laugh,
Stop it! You're Stupid! It's always my fault but if only they knew half...

Half of what I go through to sit and hear and learn,
Half of what I go through when I can't concentrate, but it's my turn.

If only I could switch it off, I wish there was a special code,
because sometimes it's not easy to live in a brain of sensory overload!

Please know

I may not get to say it often, but I'm blessed to
have you in my life,
For all the care you show, the perspective you
bring, for not judging me when I'm in strife.

I may not say it often but I'm grateful for you,
you exactly as you turn up,
For knowing you trust me enough to be yourself,
continues to fill my cup.

I may not say it often, but I have a purpose
because of you,
For seeing you believe in me, gives me the
courage to see my dreams and pursue.

I may not say it often but I feel loved because
you see,
because despite my doubts and insecurities, you
still remind me I'm me!

I may not say it often but please always know,
that I am thankful and turn up with purpose and
love each day,
because of you being you in exactly your own
way!

Adventures

Sometimes adventure is that big trip away,
but sometimes adventure is looking for
excitement in each day.

Sometimes adventure is seeing each day as a
new possibility,
to go, see, do or learn, something new about me.

Sometimes adventure goes deep inside,
deep in our hearts to see where we are and what
we try and hide.

Sometimes adventure is a book, movie, story or
podcast,
something to escape life and make feeling
adventurous last.

Sometimes adventure is trying something new,
that scares yet excites us at the thought of what
we can do.

Sometimes adventure is simply waking up each
day,
with curiosity and eagerness for what might
come your way.

Adventure lies within each heart that chooses to
create and feel,
So look within yourself and today your
adventure could be surreal!

Waiting

Sit, clock, scroll, breath
Pace, stand, sit seath.
Feeling forgotten, lonely and unloved
wishing I could fade away or set sail like a dove

not wanting to feel alone and insignificant,
not wanting to lose myself and cry or yell or rant
holding on to hope that I'm not a forgotten entity
holding onto whatever is left of my identity

realising that waiting is letting someone else
hold
the power in my thoughts of self and how I see
my life unfold
I do know my worth, it doesn't wait for you
but I am allowed to be hurt because of what you
do.

There's another day

Their thoughts in mind,
Try to seek knowledge to find
The answer that will keep,
Them from taking the leap.

The hope that will give,
The thought they can live,
To get through the despair
To know that love is there.

To find inner peace,
To stand up at the crease,
To believe in another day,
To know there is a way.

The strength they have within,
To see the battle they can win,
The courage to face the end,
To see change is around the bend.

To know that despite of the numb,
There is something that can be done,
That tomorrow will be new,
That today you will get through!

You are more!

You are more than you think, You are more than
you feel,
You are more than what you think makes you
seem real.

You are more than the sum of what happened
today,
You are more than the thoughts that keep you at
bay.

You are more than you know, You are more than
you see,
You are more than what you believe yourself to
be.

You are more than the total of what you can do,
You are more than the negativity that keeps
seeping through.

You are more than you say, You are more than
you hear,
You are more than the disbelief that keeps you in
fear.

You are more than the thoughts your head is
telling you,
You are more, you are your light and you will
keep shining through!

Remember

We forget the simplicity of the sun, the warmth
on our face,
Of the enveloping sense of comfort that comes
from a soft embrace.

We forget the awe of the night, the sparkling
guiding star,
Of the enriching connection that this world
gives, no matter how near of far.

We forget the presence of the small singing
birds, the hard-working ants,
Of the cycling of nature and the seeds in which
one plants.

We forget the wonder of this world, the beauty
all around,
Of the engulfing sense of amazement that can
come from the tiniest sound.

We forget the goodness in each day, and what
each moment can bring,
Of the enduring sense of purpose, when you
remember and let your heart sing!

I Love You

21

I have you,
I hold you,
I feel you.

I need you,
I want you,
I choose you.

I touch you,
I hear you,
I see you.

I trust you,
I know you,
I love you.

Choose wisely!

As I sit and reflect on the blessings I receive,
It gives me something greater in which I believe.

Something bigger to belong to, with which I
connect,
That reminds me I am enough when myself I
neglect.

Those people that surround me, that fill and
complete my heart,
That give me a sense of purpose, like I feel I
play an important part.

A part in something greater, than what I thought
I could ever be,
A family of my choosing, but one who also
chooses me!

The Music in Me

Today I get this chance to play, because I chose
to play, because I know the joy it brings to me,
the sense of calm and clarity.

To connect to something greater and just let your
emotions flow, to give in to control and just go
where I need to go.

To trust that today will be all it needs to be and
with it, it brings me so much opportunity.

That I can sit in my emotions and let the music
seep, to stop the negativity that inside me tries to
creep.

Today I choose to lean into the keys, lean into
the music, lean in to me and all the possibilities
that I get to see and be

You Make a Difference

As the sun tilts its head and starts to sail away,
I hope you remember you made a difference
today.

A big or small difference, it does not matter the
size,
It's the joy you bring to others, that's truly your
greatest prize.

Thank You

Thank you for being you, for all you are to me.
For the comfort, warmth, encouragement and
hospitality.

Thank you for being you, for all the love you
give,
For making me realise in times of doubt, that I
have meaning to live.

Thank you for being you, for all that you
selflessly do,
For reminding me I am worth loving and even
cherishing too.

Thank you for being you, for all that you make
me see,
For reminding me that life is better with true,
trusting company.

Odd!

Twenty-one, an odd number, it doesn't sit
comfortable with me.
Oops! I'm starting to show some of the little
things that show my vulnerability.

The oddness of the number, to add it only makes
three.
Is it weird that I prefer even, are there others or
is it only me?

Writing this poem seems odd because it is odd,
as odd as it can be,
However I have made it to the end and
challenged my insecurity.